Sam the Guardian Angel

Illustrations by Theresa Hossenlopp.

Graphic design by Caroline Green.

ISBN: 978-1-5051-1601-4

Published in the United States by
TAN Books
P. O. Box 267
Gastonia, NC 28053
www.TANBooks.com
Printed and bound in the United States of America

Sam the Guardian Angel

Lis Luwia
Illustrated by Theresa Hossenlopp

TAN Books
Gastonia, North Carolina

"Hi! I'm Angie and this is my guardian angel. He goes everywhere with me, and he's my best friend!"

"Hi! I'm Sam! I love spending time with Angie. She is so special to me!"

Did You Know?

Every person has a guardian angel assigned to watch over and protect him or her!

“Sam knows a lot of things about the Catholic faith because guardian angels are God’s special helpers. He comes straight from God to help me. Isn’t that amazing?”

Did You Know?

God wants you to be closer to him and to feel his love so angels do whatever they can to bring you closer to him and to show you his love.

"Your guardian angel
wants to help you too.
All you have to do is ask!"

"Today, I asked Sam to help me during Mass. Sometimes there are things during Mass that I don't understand. I know Mass is important, but I'm not sure how it is important."

"Look, there's the church! Let's go in."

Did You Know?

The Catechism says that through Mass we unite ourselves with the heavenly liturgy and look forward to eternal life. Essentially, Mass is the closest we will ever get to heaven while on earth!

"Sam, none of my friends are here today. That makes me a little sad."

"Do you know what's special about being Catholic? We all belong to the same Church and God is our Father. Since we all have the same Father, that means we are brothers and sisters in Christ! All of these people in church are related to you through our Holy Church!"

"Wow, that is so amazing! I never thought about all of the other people. It makes greeting them before Mass seem more special!"

Did You Know?

The brotherhood and sisterhood you share with other Catholics lasts beyond death. That's why we can ask the saints to pray for us in heaven—it's called the communion of saints! We're all connected because of our Father!

"Sam, I really want to sing with everyone, but I don't know the words."

"Singing for God is amazing! Do you hear all of the voices in this church singing about God's glory? All of the guardian angels are singing too!

"Just try to follow along. You'll remember the words in no time! You can always ask your parents for help with the songs at home. Just remember you're singing for God, so you can always sing quietly, 'Jesus, I love you,' during the songs and he would love that!"

Did You Know?

The Catechism says that singing in Mass is a great treasure and considered more valuable than any other art.

"It's really hard for me to sit still and Mass is so long!"

"It is hard when you don't understand. As you start to see and understand more during Mass, then it won't seem so long. Try to pick up on the things you remember from Mass last week, and if you are really confused or bored, just close your eyes and pray to God. He just wants to be with you, especially when you're in his house."

Did You Know?

The very first Mass was held by Jesus on Holy Thursday before he was crucified. Think about how special we are to get to experience Mass today because of what Jesus did for us!

I love you Jesus... ...I am here.

"I can do that! But I don't really hear God talk back to me. How do I know he hears me?"

"God knows everything. You make him so happy when you pray. Don't worry and just love him!"

Did You Know?

God does speak to us, but sometimes we can't hear him or he answers our prayers later on. Just tell him, "Speak Lord, your servant is listening" often and spend time with him in prayer. He will answer you.

"This part is really different. Why are we on our knees?"

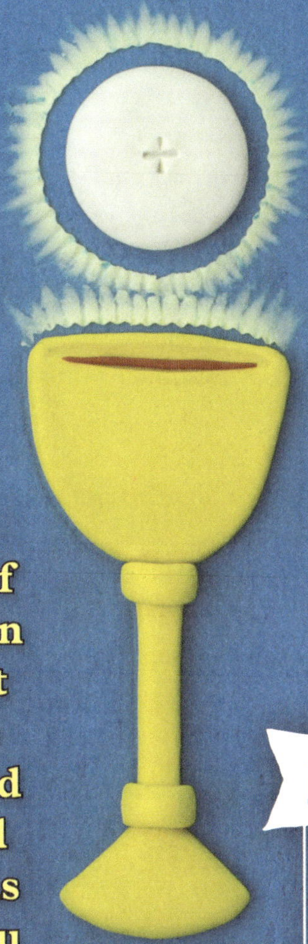

"This is when Jesus comes! He makes himself available for you, to live in you and help you live out what he wants you to do everyday. I wish you could see what I see, Angie! All of the angels are so joyous right now! We all want you to participate in Christ this way; it is the closest thing to heaven on earth."

Did You Know?

Jesus is fully present in the Eucharist and he wants to live inside of you. Try to keep your heart clean of sin and love him to make your heart a beautiful place for him to rest.

"I really like shaking everyone's hand during this part. It's fun!"

"Do you know why we say 'Peace be with you?' It's a blessing of peace to others and Jesus said the same thing when he was on earth!"

Did You Know?

Jesus came to his disciples after he resurrected and greeted them by saying "Peace be with you." Can you try to say that to someone this week outside of Mass? Isn't peace a beautiful thing to wish for someone?

"I really want to receive Jesus in the Holy Eucharist!"

"You will, and Jesus wants you to as well! Until you make your First Communion, make a spiritual communion with him by offering your heart and soul as a place for him to live."

Did You Know?

If you aren't able to make it to daily Mass or you can't receive Eucharist, say this Act of Spiritual Communion Prayer written by St. Alphonsus de Liguori. Even after you receive your First Communion you can say this beautiful prayer:

My Jesus, I believe that You are present in the Most Holy Sacrament. I love You above all things, and I desire to receive You into my soul. Since I cannot at this moment receive You sacramentally, come at least spiritually into my heart. I embrace You as if You were already there and unite myself wholly to You. Never permit me to be separated from You. Amen.

"Mass is ending and I don't understand what the priest is saying. What does he want me to do?"

"Great question, Angie! He wants you to go out and bring peace and Jesus's love to the people you meet everyday. Jesus gives you the strength to be able to do this. So, if you're shy or nervous, just ask for Jesus's help!"

Did You Know?

The word "Mass" actually comes from the Latin phrase "Ite, missa est," which means "Go, it is sent." This means that Mass is actually a sending forth of believers into the world; we are sent forth with a purpose: to spread God's love! And *that's* why we say, "Thanks be to God!" at the end of Mass.

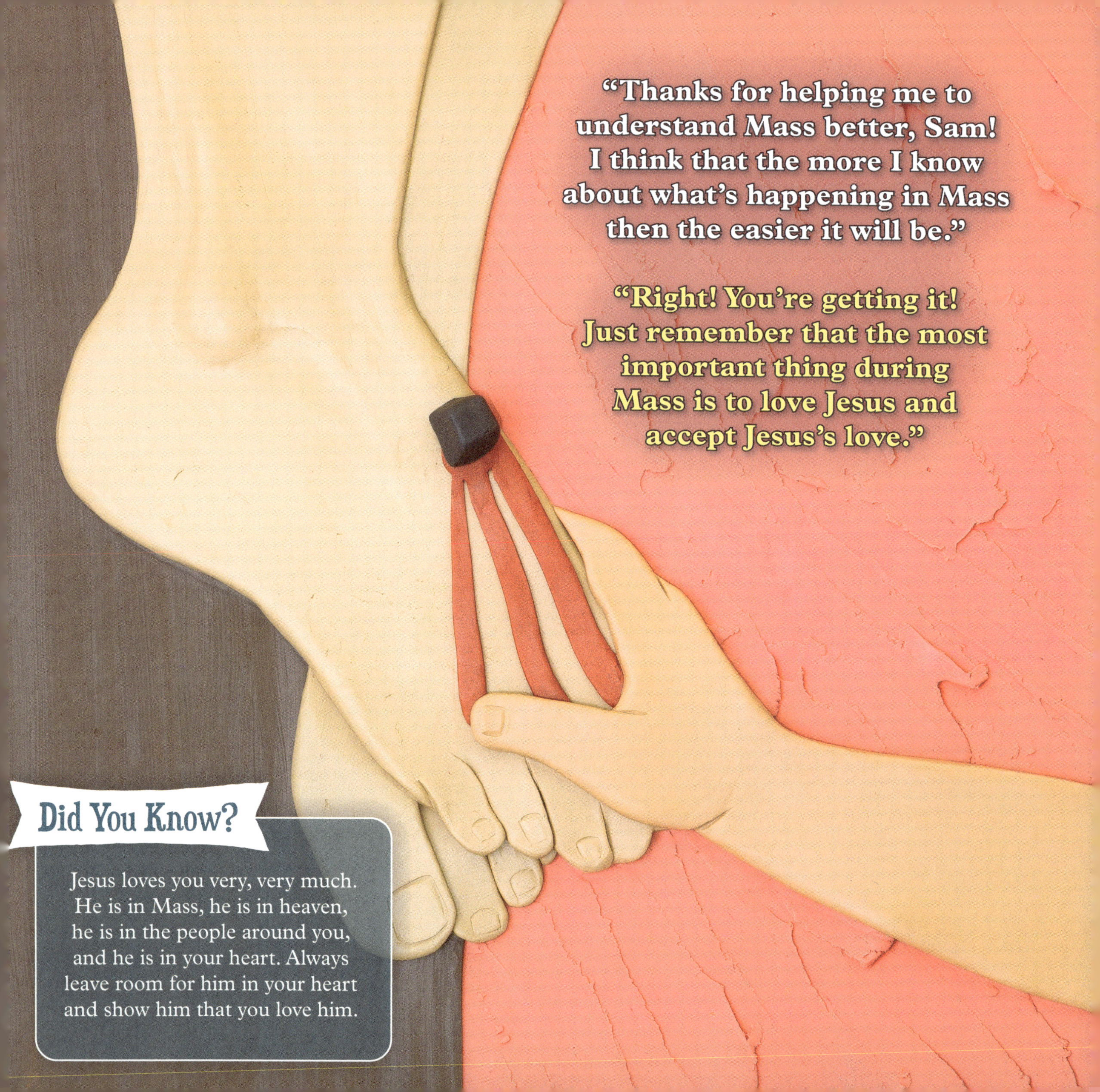

"Thanks for helping me to understand Mass better, Sam! I think that the more I know about what's happening in Mass then the easier it will be."

"Right! You're getting it! Just remember that the most important thing during Mass is to love Jesus and accept Jesus's love."

Did You Know?

Jesus loves you very, very much. He is in Mass, he is in heaven, he is in the people around you, and he is in your heart. Always leave room for him in your heart and show him that you love him.

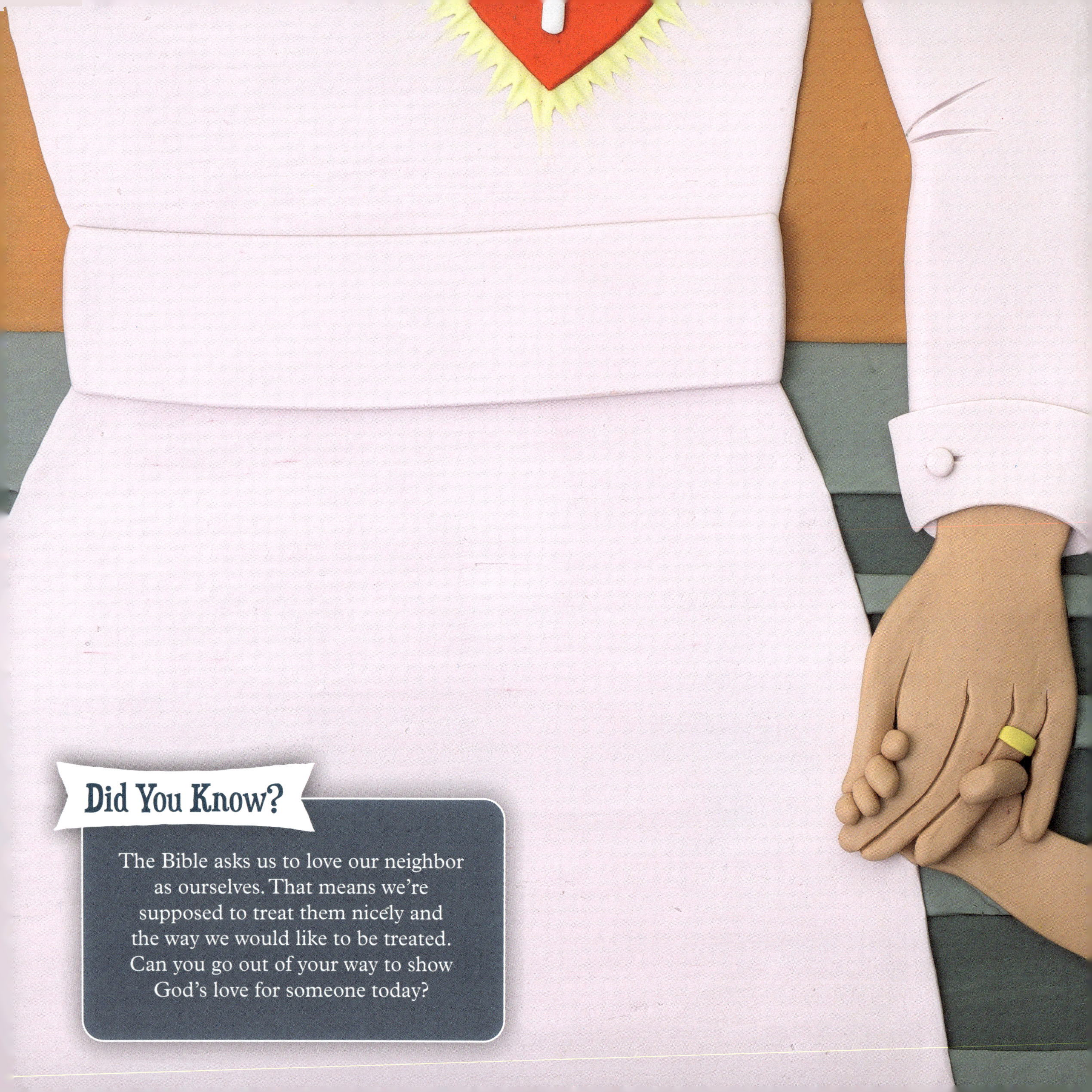

Did You Know?

The Bible asks us to love our neighbor as ourselves. That means we're supposed to treat them nicely and the way we would like to be treated. Can you go out of your way to show God's love for someone today?

"We are also called to take Jesus's love and share it with others. Do you think you can do that?"

"YES!"

Angel of God,
my Guardian
dear, to whom
God's love
commits me
here, ever this
day be at my
side, to light
and guard, to
rule and guide.
Amen.

About the Author

Lis Luwia has written several books, including *My Catholic Prayer Journal* and *Embracing the Cross: A Catholic Devotional*. She also runs the Catholic events website DioceseEvents.com. She and her husband have 3 children and live in the Midwest. Lis spends her days homeschooling her children, loves the sound of her children's laughter and enjoys the smell of freshly baked bread. Dig up more of Lis' work at LisLuwia.com.

About the Illustrator

Theresa Hossenlopp has a BFA in Illustration from Rochester Institute of Technology in Upstate New York. She worked in Stop Motion Animation after college. She now lives in NE Ohio with her super supportive husband and four creative children. Theresa spends much of her time homeschooling her kids, helping them learn their Catholic faith, and teaching art classes. She enjoys dates with her husband, hikes in the woods and planting in her garden. This is Theresa's first illustrated children's book. The illustrations were made using plasticine clay.

Special Thanks

Thank you to those who modeled for the characters in this book and also to Loren Nauth of Lakehouse Photography.